THE FATHER

by Florian Zeller

Translated by
Christopher Hampton

USE OF COPYRIGHTED MUSIC

A licence issued by Concord Theatricals to perform this play does not include permission to use the incidental music specified in this publication. In the United Kingdom: Where the place of performance is already licensed by the PERFORMING RIGHT SOCIETY (PRS) a return of the music used must be made to them. If the place of performance is not so licensed then application should be made to PRS for Music (www.prsformusic.com.). A separate and additional licence from PHONOGRAPHIC PERFORMANCE LTD.(www. ppluk.com) may be needed whenever commercial recordings are used. Outside the United Kingdom: Please contact the appropriate music licensing authority in your territory for the rights to any incidental music.

USE OF COPYRIGHTED THIRD-PARTY MATERIALS

Licensees are solely responsible for obtaining formal written permission from copyright owners to use copyrighted third-party materials (e.g., artworks, logos) in the performance of this play and are strongly cautioned to do so. If no such permission is obtained by the licensee, then the licensee must use only original materials that the licensee owns and controls. Licensees are solely responsible and liable for clearances of all third-party copyrighted materials, and shall indemnify the copyright owners of the play(s) and their licensing agent, Concord Theatricals Ltd., against any costs, expenses, losses and liabilities arising from the use of such copyrighted third-party materials by licensees.

IMPORTANT BILLING AND CREDIT REQUIREMENTS

If you have obtained performance rights to this title, please refer to your licensing agreement for important billing and credit requirements.

THE FATHER, in this translation by Christopher Hampton, was commissioned by the Ustinov Studio, Theatre Royal Bath, and first presented on 16 October 2014. The cast was as follows:

ANDRÉ	Kenneth Cranham
ANNE	Lia Williams
PIERRE	Colin Tierney
LAURA	Jade Williams
MAN	Brian Doherty
WOMAN	Rebecca Charles

Directed by James Macdonald
Designer Miriam Buether
Lighting Designer Guy Hoare
Sound Designer Christopher Shutt

This production transferred to the Tricycle Theatre, London, on 7 May 2015, with Claire Skinner in the role of Anne and Jim Sturgeon as the Man.

Le Père in its original French production was first presented at the Théâtre Hébertot, Paris, on 30 September 2012. This production was revived on 17 January 2015.

CHARACTERS

ANNE
ANDRÉ
MAN
WOMAN
LAURA
PIERRE

One

ANDRÉ*'s flat.*

ANNE So? What happened?

ANDRÉ Nothing.

ANNE Dad.

ANDRÉ What?

ANNE Tell me.

ANDRÉ I just did. Nothing happened.

ANNE Nothing happened?

ANDRÉ Nothing at all. Just you bursting in on me as if something had happened, something... But nothing happened. Nothing at all.

ANNE Nothing happened?

ANDRÉ Nothing.

ANNE I've just had her on the phone.

ANDRÉ So? What does that prove?

ANNE She left in tears.

ANDRÉ Who?

ANNE You can't go on behaving like this.

ANDRÉ It's my flat, isn't it? I mean, this is incredible. I've no idea who she is, this woman. I never asked her for anything.

ANNE She's there to help you.

ANDRÉ To help me do what? I don't need her. I don't need anyone.

ANNE She told me you'd called her a little bitch. And I don't know what else.

ANDRÉ Me?

ANNE Yes.

ANDRÉ Could be. I don't remember.

ANNE She was in tears.

ANDRÉ What, just because I called her...

ANNE No. Because you... Apparently you...

ANDRÉ Me?

ANNE Yes. With a curtain rod.

ANDRÉ With a curtain rod... What is this nonsense?

ANNE That's what she told me. She told me you threatened her. Physically.

ANDRÉ This woman is raving mad, Anne. With a curtain rod... Can you see me doing that? I mean... Obviously she has no idea what she's talking about. Physically? With a... No, best if she does leave, believe me. She's raving mad. Best if she does leave. Believe me. Especially as...

ANNE As what?

ANDRÉ Mm? Listen... If you must know, I suspect she was...

ANNE She was?

ANDRÉ She was...

ANNE She was what?

ANDRÉ *(whispering)* I didn't want to tell you, but I suspect she was...

ANNE *(impatiently)* She was what, Dad?

ANDRÉ She was stealing from me.

ANNE Isabelle? Of course not. What are you talking about?

ANDRÉ I'm telling you. She stole my watch.

ANNE Your watch?

ANDRÉ Yes.

ANNE Isn't it more likely you just lost it?

ANDRÉ No, no, no. I already had my suspicions. So I set a trap for her. I left my watch somewhere, out in the open, to see if she'd pinch it.

ANNE Where? Where did you leave it?

ANDRÉ Mm? Somewhere. Can't remember. All I know is it's now nowhere to be found. Nowhere to be found. I can't find it, there's your proof. That girl stole it from me. I know it. So yes, maybe I called her a... Like you say. It's possible. Maybe I got a bit annoyed. All right. If you like. But, really, Anne, a curtain rod, steady on... Raving mad, I'm telling you.

ANNE sits down. She looks winded.

What's the matter?

ANNE I don't know what to do.

ANDRÉ What about?

ANNE We have to talk, Dad.

ANDRÉ That's what we're doing, isn't it?

ANNE I mean, seriously.

Pause.

This is the third one you've...

ANDRÉ I said, I don't need her! I don't need her or anyone else! I can manage very well on my own!

ANNE She wasn't easy to find, you know. It's not that easy. I thought she was really good. A lot of good qualities. She... And now she doesn't want to work here any more.

ANDRÉ You're not listening to what I'm telling you. That girl stole my watch! My watch, Anne! I've had that watch for years. For ever! It's of sentimental value. It's... I'm not going to live with a thief.

ANNE *(exhaustedly)* Have you looked in the kitchen cupboard?

ANDRÉ What?

ANNE In the kitchen cupboard. Behind the microwave. Where you hide your valuables.

Pause.

ANDRÉ *(horrified)* How do you know?

ANNE What?

ANDRÉ How do you know?

ANNE I just know, that's all. Have you looked there for your watch?

ANDRÉ Mm? Yes. I... I think so.

He frowns.

ANNE Dad, you have to understand I can't come every day. It's...

ANDRÉ Who's asking you to?

ANNE It's the way it is. I can't leave you on your own.

ANDRÉ What are you talking about? You're just being insulting.

ANNE No, it's not insulting. You have to accept the idea that you need someone. If only to do your shopping. Not to mention... the other stuff. I'm not going to be able to do it any more.

ANDRÉ Have you been in my cupboard?

ANNE What?

ANDRÉ Anne. Tell me the truth. Have you been in my cupboard?

ANNE No.

ANDRÉ Then how do you know that... I mean...that I sometimes... with my valuables...when I... Yes. In short. How do you know?

ANNE I can't remember. I must have opened it by accident.

ANDRÉ *looks appalled. He hurries off towards the kitchen.*

Where are you going?

He exits.

I didn't touch anything, Dad. Don't worry. Can you hear me? Dad? I didn't touch anything. *(Almost to herself)* We can't go on like this. We just can't. Not like this... It's impossible... Why can't you understand?

He comes back. He's holding his watch.

You found it?

ANDRÉ Found what?

ANNE Your watch.

ANDRÉ Oh. Yes.

ANNE You realise Isabelle had nothing to do with it.

ANDRÉ Only because I hid it. Luckily. Just in time. Otherwise I'd be here talking to you with no means of knowing what time it was. It's five o'clock, if you're interested. Myself, I am interested. Pardon me for breathing. I need to know exactly where I am during the day. I've always had this watch, you know. If I were to lose it, I'd never recover.

ANNE Have you taken your pills?

ANDRÉ Yes. But why are you... You keep looking at me as if there was something wrong. Everything's fine, Anne. The world is turning. You've always been like that. A worrier. Even when there's no reason. You're like your mother. Your mother was like that. Always scared. Always looking for reasons to be scared. But that's not the way the world works. All right, fine... You'll tell me there's also a kind of... That the shadows are closing in. But mostly, *no*. You see what I'm saying? That's what you have to understand. Now your sister, she's always been much more...much less... She doesn't keep worrying about everything. I mean, she leaves me be. Where is she, by the way?

ANNE I'm going to have to move, Dad.

ANDRÉ Move, you mean...

ANNE Live somewhere else.

ANDRÉ Right. Why not. Sounds good.

ANNE I'm going to have to leave Paris.

ANDRÉ Really? Why?

ANNE We talked about this. Do you remember?

Brief pause.

ANDRÉ Is that why you're so keen on this nurse living with me? Is that the reason, Anne?

Brief pause.

Well, obviously it is. The rats are leaving the ship.

ANNE I won't be here, Dad. You need to understand that.

ANDRÉ You're leaving?

Pause.

But when? I mean...why?

ANNE I've met somebody.

ANDRÉ You?

ANNE Yes.

ANDRÉ You mean...a man?

ANNE Yes.

ANDRÉ Really?

ANNE You needn't sound so surprised.

ANDRÉ No, it's just that...since your... What was his name?

ANNE Antoine.

ANDRÉ That's right. You have to admit, since Antoine, there hasn't been a lot of... What's he do, anyway?

ANNE He lives in London. I'm going to go and live there.

ANDRÉ What, you? In London? You're not going to do that, are you, Anne? I mean, come off it... Never stops raining in London!

Pause.

Do I know him?

ANNE Yes. You've met him.

ANDRÉ Are you sure?

ANNE Yes, Dad. Lots of times.

ANDRÉ Oh?

Pause. He's trying to remember.

So, if I understand correctly, you're leaving me. Is that it? You're abandoning me...

ANNE Dad...

ANDRÉ What's going to become of me?

Pause.

Why can't he come and live in Paris?

ANNE He works over there.

ANDRÉ What about your job?

ANNE I can work from home. I don't need to be in Paris.

ANDRÉ I see.

ANNE You know, it's important to me. Otherwise, I wouldn't be going. I... I really love him.

Pause. He says nothing.

I'll come back and see you often. At weekends. But I can't leave you here all on your own. It's not possible. That's why. If you refuse to have a carer, I'm going to have to...

ANDRÉ To what?

Pause.

To what?

ANNE You have to understand, Dad.

ANDRÉ You're going to have to what?

She lowers her eyes. Pause.

...You're going to have to *what*?

Pause.

Blackout.

Two

Same room. **ANDRÉ** *is alone.*

ANDRÉ I've got to find that lawyer's number. And call him. Yes. I haven't lived all these years to be treated like a...like this. No. I've got to phone... Yes. A lawyer. My own daughter... My own daughter...

A **MAN** *suddenly appears.*

MAN Everything all right?

ANDRÉ Sorry?

MAN Everything all right?

ANDRÉ What are you doing?

MAN Sorry?

ANDRÉ What are you doing here? What are you doing in my flat?

MAN André, it's me... Pierre.

ANDRÉ What?

MAN Don't you recognise me? It's me, Pierre...

ANDRÉ Who? What are you doing here?

MAN I live here.

ANDRÉ You?

MAN Yes.

ANDRÉ You live here?

MAN Yes.

ANDRÉ You live in my flat? That's the best yet. What is this nonsense?

MAN I'm going to phone Anne.

He moves towards the telephone.

Your daughter...

ANDRÉ Thank you, yes, I do know who Anne is! Do you know her?

Brief pause.

You a friend of hers?

No answer.

I'm speaking to you. Do you know Anne?

MAN I'm her husband.

ANDRÉ *(caught off guard)* You are?

MAN Yes.

ANDRÉ Her husband? But... Since when?

MAN Coming up for ten years.

He dials a number.

ANDRÉ *(trying to conceal his dismay)* Ah, yes. Of course. Yes, yes. Obviously. Ten years, already? Time passes at such a lick... But I thought... Didn't you, aren't you separated?

MAN Who? Anne and me?

ANDRÉ Yes. You aren't?

MAN No.

ANDRÉ Are you sure? I mean, I mean... Are you sure?

MAN Yes, André.

ANDRÉ But this thing about England? Wasn't she supposed to be going to London to...wasn't she?

MAN *(on the phone)* Hello, darling. Yes, it's me. Tell me. Will you be done soon? No, no problem. It's just your father isn't feeling very well. I think he'd like to see you. Yes. All right. Fine, we'll wait for you. See you. Yes. Don't be too long. No, no. Lots of love.

He hangs up.

She'll be here soon. She's just out shopping. She's coming straight back.

ANDRÉ She told me she was going to go and live in London. She told me the other day.

MAN In London?

ANDRÉ Yes.

MAN What was she going to do in London?

ANDRÉ She's met an Englishman.

MAN Anne?

ANDRÉ Yes.

MAN I don't think so, André.

ANDRÉ Yes, she has. She told me the other day, I'm not an idiot. She told me she was moving. To go and live with him. I even remember telling her it was a stupid idea, because it never stops raining in London. Don't you know about this?

MAN No.

ANDRÉ Oops.

MAN What?

ANDRÉ Have I put my foot in it?

Brief pause.

(to himself) I've put my foot in it.

MAN No, no, don't worry. She hasn't mentioned it to me, but I'm sure she was intending to soon...

ANDRÉ You didn't know anything about the Englishman?

MAN *(amused)* No.

ANDRÉ Oops-a-daisy...

Pause. He puts a hand on the **MAN***'s shoulder.*

Never mind. Chin up. Anyway, they all end up leaving sooner or later. I speak from experience.

Brief pause.

MAN You want something to drink while we're waiting for her? Glass of water? Fruit juice?

ANDRÉ No, but I mean... What was I going to say? Oh, yes, that's it, it's come back to me.

MAN What?

ANDRÉ It's because of that girl...

MAN What girl?

ANDRÉ You know, that nurse...

MAN Laura?

ANDRÉ I've forgotten her name. That girl your wife insists on handing me over to. A nurse. You know about this? As if I wasn't able to manage on my own... She told me I needed the help of this... When I can manage perfectly well on my own. Even if she had to go abroad. I don't understand why she persists in... Look at me. No, take a good look at me...

He's trying to remember the name.

MAN Pierre.

ANDRÉ That's right, Pierre. Take a good look at me. I can still manage on my own. Don't you think? I'm not completely... Mm? You agree? I'm not... *(He hunches over like an old man)* Am I? You agree? Look, I still have the use of my arms, see? *(He illustrates this capability)* And my legs. And my hands. In fact, it all works wonderfully. You agree? Of course you agree. But her? I don't know where this obsession comes from. This stupid obsession, it's ridiculous. Ridiculous. In truth, she's never known how to evaluate a situation. Never. That's the problem. She's always been that way. Ever since she was little. Thing is, she's not very bright. Not very... You agree? Not very intelligent. She gets that from her mother.

MAN I think she tries to do the best she can for you, André.

ANDRÉ The best she can, the best she can... I never asked her for anything. She's cooking up something against me, I don't know what it is. But she's cooking something up. She's cooking something up, that I do know. I suspect she wants to put me in a home for... Yes, she does. For... *(He pulls a face representing an old man)* I've seen the signs. That's what she has at the back of her mind. She almost came out with it the other day. But let me make something absolutely clear: I'm not leaving my flat! I'm not leaving it!

MAN This isn't your flat, André.

ANDRÉ Sorry?

MAN If you remember, you moved here, I mean you moved to our place while you were waiting for...

ANDRÉ What?

MAN Yes. While you were waiting for a new carer to be found... Because you quarrelled with the last one... With Isabelle.

ANDRÉ Did I?

MAN Yes. Don't you remember? That's why you're staying in our place. While you wait.

Pause. ANDRÉ *looks slightly lost.*

ANDRÉ So, Antoine...

MAN Pierre.

ANDRÉ Yes. So you're telling me, I'm in your place?

MAN Yes.

ANDRÉ *laughs and rolls his eyes.*

ANDRÉ Now I've heard everything.

The door opens. A WOMAN *enters carrying a shopping bag. It's not* ANNE.

WOMAN There, I was as quick as I could be. Everything all right? What's happening?

MAN Nothing much. Your father seemed a bit confused. I think he wanted to... Didn't you? Wanted to see you.

WOMAN Something wrong? Are you all right, Dad?

He doesn't recognise her.

Dad?

ANDRÉ I...

WOMAN Yes?

ANDRÉ What is this nonsense?

WOMAN What are you talking about?

ANDRÉ Where's Anne?

WOMAN Sorry?

ANDRÉ Anne. Where is she?

WOMAN I'm here, Dad, I'm here.

She realises he doesn't recognise her. She looks anxiously at the MAN.

I went to do some shopping. And now I'm back. I'm here, everything's all right.

ANDRÉ I... I see... But... What did you buy?

WOMAN A chicken. Sound good? Are you hungry?

ANDRÉ Why not?

He seems lost. And gloomy.

MAN Look, let me have it. I'll go and fix everything.

WOMAN Thanks.

He takes the bag and steps out into the kitchen. Pause.

Pierre called me. He said you weren't feeling very well?

ANDRÉ I feel fine. Except... There's something that doesn't make sense... About all this, I mean.

WOMAN What?

ANDRÉ It's difficult to explain. It's difficult. You wouldn't understand.

WOMAN Try me.

ANDRÉ No!

Pause.

WOMAN You look worried.

ANDRÉ Me?

WOMAN Yes. You look worried. Is everything all right?

ANDRÉ Everything's fine. It's just...

WOMAN Just what?

ANDRÉ *(annoyed)* I was just sitting there. Sitting quietly in the drawing room looking for a telephone number, and suddenly your husband arrived and...

WOMAN Who?

ANDRÉ Your husband.

WOMAN What husband?

ANDRÉ Mm? Well, yours, my dear. Not mine.

WOMAN Antoine?

ANDRÉ Your husband.

WOMAN Dad, I'm not married.

ANDRÉ Sorry?

WOMAN I got divorced more than five years ago. Have you forgotten?

ANDRÉ What? Well, then, who's he?

WOMAN Who?

ANDRÉ Are you doing this on purpose? I'm talking about... him. Who just left with the chicken.

WOMAN The chicken? What are you on about, Dad?

ANDRÉ Right here, just a minute ago. Did you not hand over a chicken to someone?

Clearly she doesn't know what he's talking about.

The chicken! A minute ago, you were holding a chicken, were you not? A chicken. A *chicken*!

WOMAN What chicken? What are you talking about, Dad?

ANDRÉ I'm worried about you, Anne.

WOMAN Me?

ANDRÉ Yes, believe me, I'm worried about you. Don't you remember? She doesn't remember. Are you having memory lapses or what? You'd better go and see someone, old girl. I'm talking about something that happened not two minutes ago. I could have timed it.

He checks his watch is still on his wrist. He's relieved.

Not two minutes ago. Yes. I could have timed it. With a chicken for dinner. Which you'd bought.

He approaches the kitchen.

WOMAN I think you're mistaken, Dad. There's no one in the kitchen.

ANDRÉ Well, that's very peculiar! He was there two minutes ago.

WOMAN Who?

He goes out for a minute.

Dad...

He comes back.

ANDRÉ He's vanished.

He looks around everywhere.

He must be hiding somewhere.

WOMAN *(smiling)* The man with the chicken?

ANDRÉ Your husband. Why are you smiling? Why are you smiling?

WOMAN Nothing. Sorry.

ANDRÉ All this nonsense is driving me crazy.

WOMAN Calm down.

ANDRÉ You want me to calm down?

WOMAN Yes. Come over here.

ANDRÉ There's something funny going on. Believe me, Anne, there's something funny going on!

WOMAN Come and sit down next to me. Come on...

He goes to sit down on the sofa. He's upset. The WOMAN *smiles at him and rests a hand on his.*

Now don't worry. Everything'll sort itself out. Mm?

ANDRÉ I don't know.

WOMAN *(tenderly)* Yes, it will. Don't worry. Have you taken your pills?

ANDRÉ What's that got to do with anything?

WOMAN Let's give you your pills. The evening dose. Then you'll feel better.

ANDRÉ It's been going on for some time. Strange things going on around us. Haven't you noticed? There was this man claiming this wasn't my flat. A really unsympathetic-looking man. A bit like your husband. Only worse. In my flat, you understand what I'm saying? It's the best yet. Don't you think? In my flat. He told me... But... This is my flat, isn't it? Mm? Anne... This is my flat?

She smiles at him without answering. She prepares his medication.

Isn't it?

Brief pause.

Tell me, Anne, this really is my flat, isn't it?

Pause. She hands him his medication. In silence.

Blackout.

Three

Simultaneously, the same room and a different room. Some furniture has disappeared: as the scenes proceed, the set sheds certain elements, until it becomes an empty, neutral space. ANNE *is alone in the room. She's on the phone.*

ANNE No, I'm expecting her any minute. I know. I hope things will work out this time. Yes. You can't imagine how...difficult it is sometimes. The other day, he didn't even recognise me. I know. I know. Lucky you were there. Yes. Yes. No, I can't see any other solution.

Suddenly, the bell rings.

Ah, there's the bell. Yes. Must be her. Yes. I... I'll say goodbye. All right. Lots of love. Me too. Me too.

She hangs up. She's on her way to answer the bell. The door opens: it's LAURA.

Hello.

LAURA Hello. Not too late, am I?

ANNE No, no. Not at all. Come in. Come in.

LAURA *enters.*

LAURA Thanks.

ANNE I was expecting you. Come in. Thanks for coming today.

LAURA That's OK.

ANNE My father's in his room. I... I'll go and fetch him. Would you like something to drink?

LAURA No, thanks.

ANNE Make yourself comfortable. I... So, yes, as I was telling you, I... He's a bit upset by the whole idea of...

LAURA That's OK.

ANNE Yes. And that can cause him to... Anyway, I think he's a bit annoyed with me. I'm telling you this just to warn you he's capable of reacting...unexpectedly.

LAURA Has he lived on his own up to now?

ANNE Yes. In a flat, not too far from here. It worked. I was able to look in on him practically every day. But eventually, we've had to come to another arrangement. It wasn't viable any more.

LAURA I understand.

ANNE He had several carers one after the other. But he had difficulty getting on with them. He has his ways... He can be quite eccentric. Yes. Quite eccentric. That's why I moved him here, in with me. I thought it'd be better for him. But I can't manage him on my own. It's too much for me. And I have to work. I have to... Yes. That's why I... Well, that's why I need someone to help me.

The door to the inner room opens. ANDRÉ *appears. He's in his pyjamas.*

ANDRÉ Did I hear the bell?

ANNE You did... Dad, I'd like you to meet Laura.

LAURA How do you do, sir.

ANNE I explained to you that Laura was going to come by today so you could meet.

ANDRÉ Hello.

LAURA Hello.

ANDRÉ You're...gorgeous.

LAURA Thank you.

ANDRÉ But I... Do we know each other? We do know each other, don't we?

LAURA No, I don't think so.

ANDRÉ Are you positive?

LAURA Yes, I think so.

ANDRÉ Your face is familiar.

LAURA Is it?

ANDRÉ Yes. Sure? I have a definite impression I've seen you before.

LAURA Maybe. I don't know.

ANNE Well. So, Laura's come by to see us to get a bit of an idea of how you live and to see to what extent she might be able to help you.

ANDRÉ I know, dear, I know that. You've already told me a hundred times. *(To* **LAURA***)* My daughter has a tendency to repeat herself. You know what it's like... It's an age thing. Would you like something to drink?

LAURA You're very kind, but no thanks.

ANDRÉ Sure? An aperitif? Must be about time for an aperitif, isn't it? What time is it? It's... Where's my...? My... Wait a minute... My... Hang on, I'll be right back.

He moves towards the kitchen and exits.

ANNE He's going to look for his watch.

LAURA Oh?

ANNE Yes. He's a very...punctual man. Even if he is in his pyjamas in the middle of the afternoon.

LAURA Perhaps he's been having a siesta.

ANNE *(a little embarrassed)* I expect so. Yes.

Pause.

LAURA In any case, he's charming.

ANNE Yes. Not always. But most of the time, yes, he's charming. Like I said, he has his ways.

LAURA Well, that's good.

ANDRÉ *returns, wearing his watch.*

ANDRÉ Just as I was saying, time for an aperitif. I have two watches. I've always had two. One on my wrist and the other in my head. It's always been that way. Would you like something, young lady?

ANNE Dad…

ANDRÉ What? I'm allowed to offer our guest something, aren't I? What would you like?

LAURA What are you going to have?

ANDRÉ A small whisky.

LAURA All right, I'll take the same.

ANDRÉ Excellent. So, two whiskys. Two! I'm not offering you one, Anne. *(To* **LAURA***)* She never drinks alcohol. Never.

ANNE It's true.

ANDRÉ Never. Not a drop. That's why she seems so…

ANNE So what?

ANDRÉ Sober. Her mother was the same. Her mother was the… soberest woman I've ever met. Whereas her little sister… It was quite another story.

LAURA You have two daughters?

ANDRÉ That's right. Even though I hardly ever hear from the other one. Élise. All the same, she was always my favourite.

Pause.

Do you ever hear from her? I don't understand why she never gets in touch. Never. Dazzling girl. A painter. An artist. Here's your whisky.

LAURA Thank you.

ANDRÉ Cheers.

They clink glasses.

I'd give everything I own for a glass of whisky. Don't you think?

LAURA Well, I don't own all that much...

ANDRÉ Don't you? What do you do for a living?

LAURA Well, I... I look after...other people.

ANDRÉ Other people?

LAURA Yes. My job is to help people who need help.

ANDRÉ *(to* ANNE*)* Sounds like one of those girls you're always trying to dump off on me.

Pause.

Must be a difficult job, isn't it? Spending all day with some... *(He makes a face signifying an invalid)* Am I right? I couldn't stand it.

LAURA What about you, what did you do for a living?

ANDRÉ I was a dancer.

LAURA Were you?

ANDRÉ Yes.

ANNE Dad...

ANDRÉ What?

ANNE You were an engineer.

ANDRÉ What do you know about it? *(To* LAURA*)* Tap dancing was my speciality.

LAURA Really!

ANDRÉ You seem surprised.

LAURA *(laughing)* Yes, a little bit.

ANDRÉ Why? Can't you imagine me as a tap dancer?

LAURA Of course. It's just... I've always loved tap dancing.

ANDRÉ You as well? I'm still great at it. I'll give you a demonstration one day.

LAURA I'd love that.

He gets up, takes a few hopeless steps. **LAURA** *starts laughing. He stops.*

ANDRÉ Why are you laughing?

LAURA *(still laughing)* It's nothing. Sorry. Sorry.

ANDRÉ *starts laughing as well.*

ANDRÉ You don't believe me?

LAURA Of course I do. It's just...

ANDRÉ Just what?

LAURA Just...the whisky.

ANDRÉ That's it, I know. I know who you remind me of. I know who she reminds me of.

ANNE Who?

ANDRÉ Élise. That's right. Élise, when she was her age.

LAURA Élise?

ANDRÉ My other daughter. The younger one. She's an angel. Don't you think?

ANNE I don't know.

ANDRÉ Yes. There's a resemblance.

ANNE Maybe. Slightly.

ANDRÉ There's a resemblance. Yes.

LAURA There is?

ANDRÉ Yes. Your habit of... That unbearable habit of laughing inanely.

Everyone stops laughing. Pause.

I had you there, didn't I? Ha ha.

Brief pause.

That's the way I am. I like taking people by surprise. It's a special brand of humour.

Brief pause.

(suddenly serious) You see, the situation's very simple. I've been living in this flat...oh, for a long time now. I'm extremely attached to it. I bought it more than thirty years ago. Can you imagine? You weren't even born. It's a big flat. Very nice. Very big. And I've been very happy here. Anyway. My daughter is very interested in it.

ANNE What are you talking about?

ANDRÉ Let me explain the situation. My daughter is of the opinion that I can't manage on my own. So she's moved in with me. Ostensibly to help me. With this man she met not long ago, just after her divorce, who has a very bad influence on her, I have to tell you.

ANNE Look, what are you talking about, Dad?

ANDRÉ And now she'd like to convince me that I can't manage on my own. The next stage will be to send me away I don't know where... Although, in fact, I do know where. *I know.* Obviously, it'll be a much more efficient way of getting hold of my flat.

ANNE Dad...

ANDRÉ But it's not going to happen that way. I may as well tell you. I have no intention of leaving any time soon. No, you heard me. I intend to outlive you. Both of you. That's right. To outlive both of you. Yes. Well, I don't know about you... But my daughter, definitely. I shall make a point of it. *I'm* going to inherit from *her*. Not the other way round. The day of her funeral, I shall give a little speech to remind everyone how heartless and manipulative she was.

ANNE I'm very sorry about this.

ANDRÉ Why? She understands completely. You're the one who doesn't understand. *(To* LAURA*)* I've been trying to explain to her for months that I can manage very well on my own. But she refuses to listen. Refuses. So since you're here and your job consists of 'helping people', perhaps you can help me to explain things clearly to her: I don't need any help from anyone and I will not leave this flat. All I want is for people to bugger off and leave me in peace. If you'd have the kindness to explain that to her, I'd be most grateful to you. There we are.

He empties his glass, gets up, brings a note out of his pocket and throws it down on the table, as if he's paying the bill.

Having said that, it was a great pleasure, I'll be leaving you.

He exits.

LAURA When you said he had his ways, you weren't kidding...

ANNE No... I'm very sorry.

ANNE *seems particularly upset.*

LAURA Don't be. That sort of reaction is quite normal.

ANNE No, I'm very sorry.

LAURA It'll all turn out fine. I'm certain of it. Don't worry.

Brief pause.

It'll all turn out fine.

ANNE You think so?

Pause. **LAURA** *drinks a mouthful of whisky.*

Blackout.

Four

ANNE *is alone. Nevertheless, she speaks as if she's talking to someone, as if she's undergoing cross-examination.*

ANNE I couldn't get to sleep. I was so tired, so tired that falling asleep was beyond me. So I got up. And I went into his room. Dad's room. He was asleep. He looked like a child. His mouth was open. He was at peace. So peaceful. And I don't know what came over me, a kind of wave of hatred, and I put my hands around his throat. Gently. I could feel his pulse beneath my hands. Like little butterflies. And then I squeezed. My hands. Squeezed them very hard... He didn't open his eyes. He didn't close his mouth. It was just living through one bad moment. One minute. Hardly that. One bad moment. Still. But it was curiously gentle. Gentle and still... When I relaxed the pressure, when I took my hands away, I sensed he was no longer breathing, that it was over at last. It was as if the butterflies had flown. Yes. He had a slight smile. He was dead. He was dead, but I had the impression he was thanking me.

Pause.

Blackout.

Five

ANNE *is laying the table for dinner, while* PIERRE *is reading the newspaper. The chicken is cooking in the kitchen.*

ANNE No, it went well. I think. She said she'd start tomorrow.

PIERRE Here?

ANNE Yes.

PIERRE Good.

ANNE Yes. Then we'll see how the first day goes. I was so afraid it wasn't going to work. But in the end it was fine. He was charming.

PIERRE There you are, you see.

ANNE Yes. She seems very sweet. Very competent. He turned on the charm for her...

PIERRE Oh, yes?

ANNE Yes. You should have seen it... He told her he'd been a dancer. A tap dancer.

PIERRE *(smiling)* No...

ANNE Yes. She started to laugh. Not in a mocking way, you understand. There was something kind about her. I was relieved. I don't know how to describe it to you. As if she was going to be able to... Well, as if the two of them were going to get on really well...

Brief pause.

He said she reminded him of Élise.

PIERRE Oh, yes? But how old is she?

ANNE I don't know. Thirty. Something like that.

PIERRE Is she pretty?

ANNE Why? Are you interested?

Pause.

PIERRE What's the matter with you?

ANNE With me?

PIERRE Yes. You seem odd. If it went well, that's good news, isn't it?

ANNE Yes, yes.

PIERRE So? What's the matter with you? Tell me.

ANNE It's just...

PIERRE What?

ANNE Just now... When he didn't recognise me... When I went down to buy the dinner... I... I don't know. It did something to me.

PIERRE I understand.

ANNE I'm finding it so hard.

PIERRE Come. Let me give you a hug.

ANNE I saw it in his eyes. He didn't recognise me. Not at all. I was like a stranger to him.

PIERRE You have to get used to it.

ANNE I can't manage to.

PIERRE I think you can, I think you're managing very well.

ANNE You're wrong. Sometimes I think I'll never manage to. And he keeps talking about Élise. I don't know what to say to him when he starts. I'm lost.

PIERRE Come here...

Brief pause.

ANNE I had a terrible nightmare last night. I dreamt I was strangling him.

Pause. She pulls herself together.

Did you put the chicken in the oven?

PIERRE Yes. It'll be ready in...in ten minutes. Hungry?

ANNE No.

Pause. She smiles at him.

Had a good day?

ANDRÉ *comes in. He sees* **PIERRE**. *He doesn't recognise him. He frowns.*

Dinner'll be ready in ten minutes, Dad. That suit you?

ANDRÉ Very good, dear. Suits me fine. Suits me... But... Hello.

PIERRE *smiles at him distractedly.*

ANNE You hungry, Dad?

ANDRÉ Yes, yes. But... We have guests this evening?

ANNE No. Why?

ANDRÉ Nothing, nothing...

ANDRÉ *stares at* **PIERRE**. *Pause.*

PIERRE *(to* **ANNE***)* Nothing special. Few meetings. Nothing special. Still waiting for Simon's answer. Always takes longer than you expect. Hopefully they'll sign before the end of the month. What about you?

ANNE I told you. Laura came by. Didn't she, Dad? Laura came to see us just now.

ANDRÉ Who?

ANNE Laura. The young woman who came to see us just now.

ANDRÉ Oh, yes.

ANNE And then I've been here ever since.

PIERRE Didn't do any work?

ANNE Not really. I've been with Dad.

ANDRÉ Has anybody seen my watch? Can't seem to find it.

ANNE Again?

ANDRÉ I've been looking for it for some time.

ANNE You must have put it in your cupboard. Don't you think? In your hiding place...

> **ANDRÉ** *starts, afraid that* **PIERRE** *has heard the word 'cupboard' and will discover his hiding place.*

ANDRÉ *(intending this for* **PIERRE***)* What are you talking about, Anne? I really don't know what you're talking about. What cupboard? Mm? There's no cupboard. No cupboard. No. I don't know what you're talking about. *(To* **ANNE***, almost a whisper)* Couldn't you be more discreet?

ANNE *(speaking more quietly)* Have you looked in your cupboard?

ANDRÉ I've just come from there. It's not there. I must have lost it somewhere. Or else it's been stolen.

ANNE No, it hasn't.

ANDRÉ *(getting annoyed, but still whispering)* What do you mean, 'No, it hasn't'? The watch must be somewhere! It can't have flown away! So why do you say 'No, it hasn't'? Why do you say that, when it very well might have been stolen? My watch.

ANNE You want me to go and look?

ANDRÉ Very much so. If it's not a bother. Because it's a worry. I'm worried. I'm losing all my things, everyone's just helping themselves. If this goes on much longer, I'll be stark naked. Stark naked. And I won't even know what time it is.

ANNE I'll be back.

> *She exits. Pause.* PIERRE *is reading his paper.* ANDRÉ
> *watches him from across the room. He clears his throat*
> *to get his attention, as one might with someone one*
> *doesn't know.*

ANDRÉ Her-hum...

> *No reaction from* PIERRE.

Her-hum...

> *No reaction.* ANDRÉ *clears his throat even more forcefully.*
> PIERRE *looks up.*

Am I disturbing you?

PIERRE Sorry?

ANDRÉ I'm not disturbing you?

PIERRE Mm? No.

> *Pause.* PIERRE *returns to his paper.*

ANDRÉ Might you have the time?

PIERRE Yes.

ANDRÉ Ah. Thanks.

> *Brief pause.* PIERRE *continues to read the paper.*

So what time is it? Exactly.

> PIERRE *looks at his watch.*

PIERRE Almost eight.

ANDRÉ That late? Shouldn't we be sitting down to dinner...?

PIERRE Yes. As soon as the chicken's ready. In ten minutes.

ANDRÉ We're having chicken this evening?

PIERRE Yes. The one Anne just bought.

ANDRÉ It's pretty, your watch. It's... It's pretty. It's... Is it yours? I mean, is it yours?

PIERRE Mm? Yes.

ANDRÉ May I see it?

Pause. PIERRE *looks up from the paper.*

PIERRE So. Apparently it went very well?

ANDRÉ Yes, very well. What?

PIERRE Well, your meeting with...the carer.

ANDRÉ Oh. Yes. Very well. Very well. She's very...

PIERRE Apparently she looks like Élise.

ANDRÉ Is that right?

PIERRE I've no idea. I've never seen her.

ANDRÉ *(still focusing on* PIERRE'*s watch)* No, it...it went well. Anne seemed pleased. You know, it's mainly for her. I don't really need... I mean, it's mainly for Anne. Might I have a look at it? Your watch...

PIERRE You're right, it's important for her that this works out. She's been worried about you, you know. It makes her very unhappy when you fall out with... Anyway, let's hope everything works out this time. Mm? That you'll be happy with this woman. That you'll welcome her a little more... warmly. What is it about my watch?

ANDRÉ Nothing. I was just looking... I wanted to check if... It's pretty. Very pretty. Did you buy it?

PIERRE Sorry?

ANDRÉ No, I mean... Was it a present or did you buy it?

PIERRE I bought it. Why?

ANDRÉ I don't suppose you kept the receipt...

PIERRE What are you talking about?

ANDRÉ For your watch.

Pause.

PIERRE I was talking about Anne.

ANDRÉ Do you know her? I mean, you... Yes, that's right, you're her... Aren't you? You're her...

Brief pause.

I'm her father. Nice to meet you. I expect we'll see a bit of each other. If you're her new... I mean, if it lasts. As for me, I can't explain why. We never really hit it off.

PIERRE *moves away from him.*

PIERRE Why are you saying that?

ANDRÉ Just telling you. We never really got on. Not like Élise. My other daughter. Now she, she was marvellous. But I haven't seen her for months. She's travelling, I think. She's going round the world. She's been very successful, I can't blame her. Painter. She's a painter. So, obviously. But I'd be so happy if she came to see me one day. I'd take her in my arms and we'd be glued to one another for hours on end, like we used to be a long time ago, when she was little and she still used to call me 'little daddy', 'little daddy'. That's what she used to call me. Nice, isn't it, 'little daddy'?

Pause. **PIERRE** *starts slowly moving towards* **ANDRÉ**.

PIERRE Can I ask you a question?

ANDRÉ Yes.

PIERRE *gets closer to him. There's something threatening about his approach.*

PIERRE But I want an honest answer. Nothing fancy... Can you do that for me?

ANDRÉ *(caught off guard)* Yes.

PIERRE Well, then...

Brief pause.

How much longer do you intend to hang around getting on everybody's tits?

Pause.

Blackout.

Six

ANNE *and* ANDRÉ. *Earlier in the day.*

ANNE I need to talk to you, Dad.

ANDRÉ Good start.

ANNE Why do you say that?

ANDRÉ My dear, when someone says 'I need to talk to you', it means they've got something disagreeable to say. Don't you find?

ANNE No. Not necessarily.

Brief pause.

ANDRÉ So? What was it you wanted to say?

ANNE *(calculating that this might not be a good time)* Never mind. Nothing.

Pause.

I've spoken to Pierre.

ANDRÉ Pierre?

ANNE Pierre, Dad. I've spoken to him.

ANDRÉ Your husband?

ANNE Dad... Pierre isn't my husband. I'm divorced.

ANDRÉ Make your mind up.

ANNE I divorced Antoine five years ago. I now live with Pierre. He's the man I'm living with.

ANDRÉ I don't care for him, that fellow. He's unsympathetic.

Brief pause.

Don't you think? I don't care for him.

ANNE He's not a fellow, Dad. He's the man I love.

Pause.

Anyway. I've spoken to him and... You remember at first, when you came to our place, it was... I mean, it was a temporary solution. You remember? It was...a stop gap. Because you'd fallen out with Isabelle. But... How shall I put this? I'm wondering if it wouldn't be better to... You're comfortable in your room, aren't you?

Brief pause.

You're comfortable in that room at the back?

ANDRÉ Yes.

ANNE Yes, you seem to be comfortable there. That's what I thought. And I was wondering if it wouldn't be more reassuring... Nicer for you if we came to a joint decision that you should move in here. I mean, for good. With us. On condition we get someone to help us.

Brief pause.

That way, we could see each other every day. It'd be easier. What do you think?

Pause.

I've spoken to Pierre about it. He agrees.

ANDRÉ But... I thought... I thought you were going to go and live in London.

ANNE No, Dad. Why do you keep going on about London? I'm staying in Paris.

ANDRÉ I don't understand any of this nonsense. You keep changing your mind. How do you expect people to keep up?

ANNE But there was never any question of going to London, Dad.

ANDRÉ Yes, there was. You told me.

ANNE I didn't...

ANDRÉ I'm sorry, Anne. You told me the other day. Have you forgotten?

Pause.

You've forgotten. Listen, Anne, I have a feeling you sometimes suffer from memory loss. You do, I'm telling you. It's worrying me. Haven't you noticed?

ANNE In any event, I'm not going to London.

ANDRÉ Good thing too. It never stops raining in London.

ANNE I'm staying here. So's Pierre.

ANDRÉ What about me?

ANNE You as well, Dad. You're staying here.

ANDRÉ What about your sister? Where's she?

ANNE Dad...

ANDRÉ What?

Brief pause.

If you knew how much I missed her...

Pause.

Blackout.

Seven

A little later in the evening. ANNE *and* PIERRE *are at the table.* ANDRÉ *is standing in the doorway to the kitchen.* ANNE *and* PIERRE *haven't noticed him.*

PIERRE He's *ill*, Anne. He's ill.

ANNE *and* PIERRE *simultaneously realise that* ANDRÉ *is in the room.* ANNE *starts. Feeling of awkwardness.*

ANNE Dad. What are you doing, standing there? Come and sit down. Come on.

He doesn't respond.

Dad...

Pause.

Come on, Dad.

Pause.

Come and sit down.

Pause.

Blackout.

Eight

Lights up almost immediately. ANNE, PIERRE *and* ANDRÉ. *A few minutes earlier in the evening. They're eating.*

PIERRE So it went well?

ANNE Yes. It went very well. Don't you agree, Dad?

ANDRÉ What?

ANNE It went well, your meeting with Laura...

ANDRÉ Yes.

ANNE You made her laugh a lot.

ANDRÉ Did I?

ANNE Yes. She thought you were charming. So she told me. She told me she thought you were charming. That you had your ways, but that you were charming. Those are the words she used. She's coming back tomorrow morning. To start working here.

Brief pause.

Like a bit more?

ANDRÉ I would. It's good, this chicken. Don't you think? Where'd you buy it?

ANNE Downstairs.

ANDRÉ Oh?

ANNE Why?

ANDRÉ No reason. It's good.

ANNE Pierre?

PIERRE No, thanks.

He pours himself another glass of wine.

Is she doing full days? I mean…

ANNE Yes. Till six.

PIERRE And then?

ANNE What d'you mean?

PIERRE After six.

ANNE I'll be there.

Pause.

PIERRE *(to* ANDRÉ, *like a criticism)* Are you satisfied?

ANDRÉ What about?

PIERRE You have a daughter who looks after you properly. Don't you? You're lucky.

ANDRÉ You're lucky too.

PIERRE You think so?

Pause. ANNE *gets up and takes the chicken into the kitchen.*

ANDRÉ What's the matter with her?

PIERRE Anne? She's tired. Needs a bit of sun.

ANDRÉ You need to look after her, old man. Why don't you go away somewhere?

PIERRE Why? You want me to tell you why?

Brief pause.

Sometimes I wonder if you're doing it on purpose.

ANDRÉ Doing what?

PIERRE Nothing.

He pours himself another glass.

We had planned to go to Corsica ten days ago.

ANDRÉ Oh?

ANNE comes back.

PIERRE Yes. But we had to cancel it at the last minute. Do you know why?

ANDRÉ No.

PIERRE Because of your row with Isabelle.

ANDRÉ Isabelle?

PIERRE The woman who was looking after you. Before Laura. Have you forgotten?

Brief pause.

We weren't able to go and leave you on your own in Paris. We had to cancel our holiday and bring you over here. And now it seems you're going to stay here. For good. If I understand correctly.

Pause.

(to **ANNE***)* He's forgotten... Amazing.

ANNE Stop it.

PIERRE What?

ANNE You're being a bit...

PIERRE A bit what?

ANNE Sarcastic.

PIERRE Not at all, Anne. I think I'm being very patient. Very patient. Believe me.

ANNE What are you trying to say?

PIERRE Nothing.

ANNE Yes, you are. Tell me.

Pause.

Why are you telling me how patient you are?

PIERRE I think anyone but me...

ANNE Yes?

PIERRE Anyone else would have pressured you to...

ANNE To what?

PIERRE To do what the situation calls for, Anne. What it calls for.

ANNE And that is?

PIERRE You know very well.

Pause.

ANDRÉ Where's the chicken? Did you take the chicken away?

ANNE Yes. Did you want some more?

ANDRÉ Yes. Is it in the kitchen?

ANNE I'll go and fetch it for you.

ANDRÉ No, it's all right, I'll go.

He gets up and goes into the kitchen. **PIERRE** *pours himself another glass of wine.*

ANNE Why do you say things like that in front of him?

PIERRE What did I say?

Pause.

Anyway, he forgets everything.

ANNE That's no reason.

Pause.

PIERRE Listen... I totally understand your feelings.

ANNE No, you don't understand.

PIERRE I do... What I don't understand is... I mean, you do so much for him. I respect you for that. You took the decision to bring him here. And why not? But... How can I put this? I honestly think you ought to come up with a different solution... He's completely lost it, Anne.

ANNE Don't talk like that.

PIERRE How do you want me to talk? I'm telling the truth. We have to find another arrangement.

ANNE Such as?

ANDRÉ appears in the doorway. He listens to the conversation. Neither of them has noticed him.

PIERRE Putting him in an institution.

ANNE A home?

PIERRE Yes. A nursing home.

Pause.

It'd be better for him.

ANNE Why are you saying this to me today? I mean, when tomorrow morning... There's this...

PIERRE Yes. You're right. We'll see. Maybe it'll work very well with this girl. You seem to think she's good. But believe me, the moment will come when... However good she is... He's *ill*, Anne. He's ill.

ANNE and PIERRE simultaneously realise that ANDRÉ is in the room. ANNE starts. Feeling of awkwardness. A repeat.

ANNE Dad. What are you doing, standing there? Come and sit down. Come on.

He doesn't respond.

Dad...

Pause.

Come on, Dad.

Pause.

Come and sit down.

He leaves without saying anything, as if he's going to bed.

Pause.

Blackout.

Nine

The room, a little later. PIERRE *is alone.* ANNE *appears in the doorway.*

PIERRE Is he asleep?

ANNE Yes. Finally.

PIERRE What a day...

ANNE Yes.

Pause.

PIERRE All right?

ANNE *(not altogether there)* He asked me to sing him a lullaby. Can you believe it? He asked me... He wanted a song. He closed his eyes right away and went to sleep. With his mouth open. He looked peaceful. So peaceful.

Brief pause.

PIERRE Did he hear? I mean...

ANNE Yes. You saw. He was there. Yes. He couldn't help hearing.

PIERRE But he didn't say anything?

ANNE No. He looked so sad. He was like a little boy. I told you, he asked me to sing him a lullaby. Brought tears to my eyes.

PIERRE I'm sure.

ANNE I remembered what sort of a man he was... I was scared of him when I was little. If you only knew. He had so much authority. And now he's here, I sing him a lullaby and he goes to sleep. I can hardly believe it. It's sad. Terribly sad.

Brief pause. She looks at PIERRE's *wine glass.*

Any left?

PIERRE Yes. Want a glass?

ANNE Please.

He gets up and pours one for her.

He was so strange this evening.

PIERRE You know what I think.

ANNE It's worrying me.

PIERRE Shall we change the subject?

ANNE Yes. Sorry.

Long pause. Sense of strain.

It's good, this wine.

PIERRE Yes.

Pause. They smile at each other. Silence. Have they nothing else to say to one another?

ANNE I've been thinking about what you said earlier on. About... When you said we should put him in a nursing home...

PIERRE Oh?

ANNE Yes. And I was thinking maybe you were right. Maybe you were right after all.

She empties her glass in one go. PIERRE *smiles at her.*

Blackout.

Ten

Still the same room, which is continuing to shed various elements. ANDRÉ *comes out of the kitchen. Morning. He's carrying a cup of coffee.*

ANDRÉ Did I sleep well? Did I sleep well? How should I know? I suppose so. Ah. I've forgotten the sugar. Sugar!

WOMAN'S VOICE *(from the kitchen)* I'll bring it.

ANDRÉ Yes. To put in the... I always take sugar in my coffee. In the mornings. I take two sugars in my coffee. It's easy, men fall into two groups. Those who take sugar in their coffee and the rest. The whole battle is to know which category you belong to. Personally, I belong to the category of those who take sugar. In their... Sorry, but that's the way I am. Right. Are you bringing the sugar?

WOMAN'S VOICE *(from the kitchen)* Yes, yes, on my way...

ANDRÉ I certainly didn't sleep well. I had a nightmare. This man turned up in my flat. I banged straight into him and he claimed it was his place. He claimed he was your husband or something along those lines. He threatened me.

He suddenly becomes aware of a new piece of furniture, one he doesn't recognise.

What's this? Who put this here? Anne? But... Anne? You might at least consult me before you... Anne?

LAURA *comes in.*

LAURA Here. I brought you the sugar.

ANDRÉ *is surprised to see her.*

ANDRÉ What?

LAURA You take two?

ANDRÉ Where's Anne?

LAURA She went out.

ANDRÉ Really? Already?

LAURA Yes.

ANDRÉ What time is it?

LAURA She'll be back soon. At the end of the day. I'm going to look for your medication.

ANDRÉ No. Wait.

LAURA What?

Brief pause. He's reluctant to let her know how surprised he is.

I'll be back. I'm just going to look for your medication.

She exits. He seems troubled by her presence.

ANDRÉ I've lost my watch again. Shit. Honestly. I... I... I should have got dressed before she arrived... I'm not very presentable. In my pyjamas.

LAURA *returns with a glass of water.*

What time is it?

LAURA Time for your medication. Here we are. Best to take them now. Then it's done. Don't you think? There are three today. This little blue one... That's the one you like. Your little blue pill. Pretty colour, isn't it?

ANDRÉ Can I ask you a question?

LAURA Yes.

ANDRÉ Are you a nun?

LAURA No.

ANDRÉ Then why are you speaking to me as if I were retarded?

LAURA Me?

ANDRÉ Yes.

LAURA But I'm not speaking to you as if you were... Not at all, I...

ANDRÉ *(imitating her)* 'Your little blue pill'. 'Your little blue pill'.

LAURA I'm sorry. I didn't think you...

ANDRÉ It's really unpleasant. You'll see when you get to my age. Which'll happen sooner than you think, by the way. It's really unpleasant.

LAURA I apologise. I... It won't happen again.

ANDRÉ *(imitating her)* 'Your little blue pill'.

She hands him the glass of water.

Have you noticed anything?

LAURA What about?

ANDRÉ What do you think? About the flat!

LAURA No. What about it?

ANDRÉ It's changed.

LAURA You think so?

ANDRÉ Yes. This piece of furniture, for instance. There. Who put that there?

LAURA I don't know. Your daughter, I imagine.

ANDRÉ Obviously. My daughter... Obviously... All the same, it's extraordinary! Not even to ask my opinion. I... Do you know what's being planned? For this flat?

LAURA No.

ANDRÉ I do. I keep my eyes open. I keep my ears open. I know everything.

Pause.

By the way, I wanted to apologise if I was a little... Last time we met... Yes, maybe I said a bit...too much... Or maybe not enough... Don't you think?

LAURA No problem. Your daughter warned me. She told me you had your ways.

ANDRÉ Oh?

LAURA *(benevolently)* Yes. And you know what my answer was?

ANDRÉ No...

LAURA I said 'Pleased to hear it'.

ANDRÉ Did you? That's nice. You look so like Élise, it's amazing. My other daughter. Not Anne, no. The other one. The one I love.

LAURA Anne told me what happened to her. I'm sorry. I didn't know.

ANDRÉ Didn't know about what?

LAURA Her accident.

ANDRÉ What accident?

LAURA What?

ANDRÉ What are you talking about?

LAURA *(hesitantly)* Nothing...

Pause.

Are you taking your medication? And then we'll go and get dressed.

ANDRÉ You see?

LAURA What?

ANDRÉ You see? What you just said...

LAURA Well...

ANDRÉ You're speaking to me as if I were retarded.

LAURA I'm not.

ANDRÉ You are!

LAURA I'm not, I...

ANDRÉ 'And then we'll go and get dressed...' 'Your little blue pill...'

Pause.

Thing is, I'm very intelligent. Very. Sometimes I even surprise myself. You need to bear that in mind, d'you understand?

LAURA Yes, I'll...bear it in mind.

ANDRÉ Thank you.

Pause.

It's true. I'm very... Sometimes I even surprise myself. Memory like an elephant.

Brief pause.

(wanting to make himself absolutely clear) You know, the animal.

LAURA Yes, yes.

He drinks his glass of water without taking his medication.

You've forgotten your pills!

He looks at them in the hollow of his hand.

ANDRÉ Oh, yes, so I did... What are they doing there?

LAURA I'll go and get you another glass of water.

ANDRÉ No, no. Don't bother. I'll swallow them with the...

LAURA What?

ANDRÉ You'll see. With the coffee.

LAURA Are you sure?

ANDRÉ Positive.

LAURA It'd be easier with the...

ANDRÉ No, it wouldn't. Look. Here. *(He begins what seems to him the equivalent of a magic trick)* You'll see. Are you watching? Watch carefully. I'll stick them in my gob. Watch, there they go, hey presto, they're in my mouth. Did you see? Did you see? Did you see?

LAURA Yes, yes. I... I'm watching.

ANDRÉ Good. And now, the coffee. Watch carefully... Hey presto.

He swallows the pills.

The job is done.

LAURA Bravo.

ANDRÉ *(modestly)* I worked in the circus for a bit when I was young.

LAURA Did you?

ANDRÉ Yes. I was quite talented. Especially at conjuring tricks. Do you like conjuring tricks? Would you like me to show you a little magic? I need a pack of cards. Do you have one?

LAURA No.

ANDRÉ There must be one in one of these drawers... We have to find it. Clubs, hearts, diamonds and spades!

He rubs his hands.

I've always liked cards. Before I was married, I often used to play with friends. Sometimes till the small hours of the morning. Hearts and spades. Place your bets! I'm going to show you a trick you've never seen. Clubs! A magic trick, invented by me. You'll see. Or rather, you won't see. You'll be blinded. Blinded!

LAURA Let's get dressed first.

ANDRÉ Now?

LAURA Yes.

ANDRÉ *(like a child)* Oh, no, not now.

LAURA Yes.

ANDRÉ Oh, no.

LAURA Yes.

ANDRÉ What's the point? I'll only have to put my pyjamas back on tonight, won't I? Might as well save some time.

LAURA I see what you mean. But if you keep your pyjamas on, we won't be able to go out.

ANDRÉ Where did you want to go?

LAURA The park. It's a nice day.

Suddenly a MAN *walks in. He also has a cup of coffee in his hand.*

MAN Everything going well?

LAURA Fine. We were going to get dressed.

ANDRÉ But...

LAURA Are you coming with me?

ANDRÉ *can't understand what this* MAN *is doing in his flat.*

MAN Everything all right, André?

ANDRÉ *is rooted to the spot. He doesn't answer.*

Something the matter?

ANDRÉ No, no...

MAN I just wanted a word with you. In fact.

ANDRÉ With me?

MAN Yes.

LAURA In that case, I'll... I'll go and get your things ready.

ANDRÉ *(alarmed)* No, wait a minute...

LAURA I'll be back.

ANDRÉ Don't leave me on my own.

LAURA What? I'll be in the next room. I'll be right back.

> **LAURA** *exits. We can see* **ANDRÉ** *is intimidated, as if this stranger's presence frightened him. Same positions and layout as Scene Five.*

MAN Can I ask you a question?

ANDRÉ Yes.

> *The* **MAN** *moves closer to him. There's something threatening about his approach.*

MAN But I want an honest answer. Nothing fancy... Can you do that for me?

ANDRÉ *(caught off guard)* Yes.

MAN Well, then...

> *Brief pause.*

How much longer do you intend to hang around getting on everybody's tits?

ANDRÉ Me?

MAN Yes, you. I'd like to know your opinion. At least, on this subject. I'm curious to know how much longer you intend to hang around getting on everybody's tits?

> *Brief pause.*

I mean, do you intend to go on ruining your daughter's life? Or is it too much to hope that you'll behave reasonably in the foreseeable future?

ANDRÉ But...what are you talking about?

MAN About you, André. About you. Your attitude.

He gives him a little slap.

ANDRÉ What are you doing? I can't allow this.

MAN You can't allow it?

ANDRÉ No.

MAN Suppose I do it again, then what will you do?

ANDRÉ I'll...

MAN Yes?

ANDRÉ You'll have to take me on. Physically.

MAN Are you saying that to tempt me?

Brief pause.

See, me as well, there's something I can't allow. Getting on everybody's tits. Past a certain age.

He smiles and gives him a second little slap.

ANDRÉ Stop it! Do you hear me? Stop this at once.

The **MAN** *still has a broad, menacing smile on his face.*
ANDRÉ*, opposite him, looks helpless.*

MAN Yes. I won't put up with that. I find that totally inappropriate. At your age.

He gives him a third little slap.

ANDRÉ Stop that! I told you to stop it!

MAN All right. I'll stop. If you're going to take it like that. But I hope I've made myself clear. That the message has come across. Otherwise, I'm going to have to...

ANDRÉ What?

Brief pause.

What?

MAN What do you think...?

He raises his hand, as if preparing to deliver another slap and **ANDRÉ** *covers his face. For a moment, he's in this humiliating defensive position. Then* **ANNE** *returns from the kitchen: the follow-on to Scene Five. Mood change. She's carrying the dish with the chicken.*

ANNE Right. I couldn't find your watch, Dad. We'll have another look later, because now the chicken's ready. We can sit down for dinner.

She sees her father.

Dad. Dad, what's the matter?

Blackout.

Eleven

Almost immediately. **ANDRÉ** *and* **PIERRE** *(in the position of the* **MAN***).* **ANNE** *comes in with the dish in her hands. A repeat.*

ANNE Right. I couldn't find your watch, Dad. We'll have another look later, because now the chicken's ready. We can sit down for dinner.

She sees her father.

Dad. Dad, what's the matter? *(To* **PIERRE***)* What's the matter with him?

PIERRE I don't know.

She puts the dish down and approaches her father, who's maintained the same position, as if afraid of being slapped.

ANNE Dad... Dad... What's the matter? Look at me. Are you all right? What is it?

ANDRÉ I...

ANNE What's the matter?

ANDRÉ *begins to sob.*

Is it because of your watch? Dad, is that the reason? We'll find it, I promise you. All right? I promise you. I haven't had the time to do a proper search yet. But we'll find it. All right? Shush. Come on, don't cry.

While she speaks, she's holding him in her arms and stroking his hair. She looks at **PIERRE** *with a concerned* *expression. Then* **PIERRE** *sits at the table. He pours himself a glass of wine.*

You'll be all right now. Mm? Shush... You'll be all right. You'll be all right. Let's eat our chicken. Shall we? You like chicken, don't you?

ANDRÉ But what time is it?

ANNE It's eight o'clock. Time to eat.

ANDRÉ Eight o'clock in the evening?

ANNE Yes, Dad.

ANDRÉ But I thought it was morning. I've only just got up. Look, I'm still in my pyjamas.

ANNE No, it's evening and I've cooked you a chicken. Come on, let's eat. Come on. Little daddy. Little daddy.

He seems very lost.

Pause.

Blackout.

Twelve

The room, a little later. ANDRÉ *is already in bed.* PIERRE *and* ANNE. *A repeat.*

ANNE Any left?

PIERRE Yes. Want a glass?

ANNE Please.

He gets up and pours one for her.

He was so strange this evening.

PIERRE You know what I think.

ANNE It's worrying me.

PIERRE Shall we change the subject?

ANNE Yes. Sorry.

Long pause. Sense of strain.

It's good, this wine.

PIERRE Yes.

Pause. They smile at each other. Silence.

ANNE I've been thinking about what you said earlier on. About...
When you said we should put him in a nursing home.

PIERRE Oh?

ANNE Yes. And I was thinking maybe you were right. Maybe
you were right, after all.

PIERRE I think I was.

ANNE It hurt me so much to see him like that this evening.

PIERRE Yes.

ANNE I had the feeling he was frightened of you.

PIERRE I know.

ANNE I'm frightened of you too.

Pause. Oddly, he smiles.

PIERRE Don't talk such nonsense. Stop being frightened. Believe me, this is the right decision. Afterwards, we'll be able to lighten up a little. Go away somewhere. Wouldn't you like to go away?

ANNE Where?

PIERRE I don't know. A long way away. Just the two of us. Live a bit...

Brief pause.

Listen to me, you have no reason to feel guilty. It doesn't make any sense.

ANNE Sense? What does make any sense?

PIERRE Being happy. Being together. Being alive.

She kisses him.

Blackout.

Thirteen

The following morning. By now the flat is practically empty. ANDRÉ *is alone. Suddenly,* ANNE *appears.*

ANNE Up already?

ANDRÉ I didn't sleep.

ANNE Last night?

ANDRÉ No. Not a wink.

ANNE Why? Aren't you feeling well?

ANDRÉ Have you seen?

ANNE What?

ANDRÉ What do you mean, 'What?' Look around you. There's no furniture.

ANNE So?

ANDRÉ So? We've been burgled.

ANNE No, we haven't.

ANDRÉ But you can see, there's nothing here!

ANNE It's always been like this, Dad. It's the way the flat is designed.

ANDRÉ Is that what you think?

ANNE Of course. It's always been like this.

ANDRÉ I'm sorry, you're wrong.

ANNE I'm not. I don't think. Don't you like it? You think it's a bit minimal?

ANDRÉ Horrible, more like. Who's done this? Who designed it?

ANNE I did, Dad.

ANDRÉ Did you? But there's nothing here.

ANNE I know. I like it like that. Right. I need a coffee. How about you?

ANDRÉ There was furniture. I remember it. There were pieces of furniture all over the place.

ANNE You're mixing it up with your flat, Dad. It's always been like this here. Right. I'm going to have a coffee. Then, we'll get dressed.

She exits.

ANDRÉ Already?

ANNE *(offstage)* Yes. You have a visitor today. Remember?

Pause.

(offstage) Dad, do you remember?

ANDRÉ My dear, you must give up this habit of repeating the same thing over and over again, it gets very boring. Burble, burble, burble. Never-ending burbling on. Of course I remember. How could I have forgotten? You never stop talking about it.

ANNE *has returned.*

ANNE I'm sorry. I just wanted to be sure you'd remembered. She shouldn't be long.

ANDRÉ This early?

ANNE Yes. She's supposed to come for your breakfast. Would you like a coffee before she...?

ANDRÉ I dreamt about her last night.

ANNE Laura?

ANDRÉ Yes. Well, I think I did. I can see her face.

ANNE *smiles at him.*

You know, she really reminded me of your sister...

ANNE Laura? Yes. That's what you said yesterday.

ANDRÉ Doesn't she remind you?

ANNE Mm? Yes, perhaps.

Pause.

Anyway, if you like her, I'm happy. She seems really nice. I mean, sweet. And efficient. She'll look after you well.

ANDRÉ Yes. I like her.

ANNE Good. We'd better get you dressed before she arrives, don't you think?

ANDRÉ Who?

ANNE Laura. Your new carer. The one you like.

ANDRÉ Ah, yes, yes, yes.

ANNE Better to have a jacket on when she arrives.

ANDRÉ And trousers.

ANNE She very much enjoyed meeting you yesterday, you know. She found you very...

ANDRÉ Very what?

ANNE I can't remember the word she used... Oh, yes. Charming. She said you were charming.

ANDRÉ Did she?

ANNE I must say, you did quite a little number on her.

ANDRÉ I did?

ANNE Yes. You convinced her you knew how to dance. That you were good at tap dancing.

ANDRÉ Me?

ANNE *(laughing)* Yes.

ANDRÉ *(a childlike smile)* And what did she say?

ANNE She said she hoped you'd give her a demonstration. One day.

ANDRÉ Funny. I didn't even know I knew how to tap dance. Did you?

ANNE No.

ANDRÉ Hidden talents.

ANNE Apparently, yes.

ANDRÉ Tap dancing?

Brief pause. He reflects. Doorbell.

ANNE Ah.

ANDRÉ Is that her?

ANNE I expect so.

ANDRÉ But...so soon? I'm not ready. I'm not dressed.

ANNE Never mind. You can get dressed later.

ANDRÉ No. I... I have to put some trousers on, Anne. Anne, I'm not properly dressed.

ANNE It doesn't matter.

ANNE is heading for the door.

ANDRÉ Yes, it does matter.

ANNE You can get dressed later. She's outside the door.

ANDRÉ Anne.

ANNE What?

ANDRÉ Don't leave me like this. I'm not properly dressed. What's she going to think of me? I have to get dressed. Where are my clothes?

ANNE Dad. Why do you always make everything so difficult? You can get dressed later. There's nothing to worry about.

ANDRÉ I'll be mortified...

ANNE No, you won't.

ANDRÉ I will. Look, I'm in my pyjamas. I have to put my trousers on.

The doorbell rings again. **ANNE** *opens the door. It's the* **WOMAN** *who appears.*

ANNE Hello.

WOMAN Hello. Not too late, am I?

ANNE No, no. Not at all. Come in. Come in.

The **WOMAN** *comes in.*

WOMAN Thank you.

ANDRÉ But...who is this?

ANNE We were expecting you. Come in. Thanks for coming so early.

ANDRÉ But, Anne... It's not her.

ANNE Dad. *(To the* **WOMAN***)* Would you like something to drink? Coffee?

WOMAN No, thanks.

ANNE Have you had breakfast? Make yourself comfortable. I...

ANDRÉ I don't want her. Where's the one I like? Where is she?

ANNE But Dad... What are you talking about? Say hello to Laura.

ANDRÉ There's something that doesn't make sense about this. It doesn't make sense!

Pause.

WOMAN Do you remember me? We met yesterday.

Pause.

We were starting to get to know one another...

Pause.

ANDRÉ *seems panicked. He takes a step backwards.*

And I told you I'd come back... Just to see the way you did things and whether I could help you...

Pause.

D'you remember?

Pause.

You don't remember?

Pause.

André? D'you remember?

Pause.

D'you remember?

Pause.

Blackout.

Fourteen

Almost immediately. No more furniture. The WOMAN
is there.

ANNE I need to talk to you, Dad.

Pause. ANDRÉ *looks frightened.*

I've spoken to Pierre.

ANDRÉ Pierre?

ANNE Pierre, Dad. I've spoken to him.

ANDRÉ I don't care for him, that fellow.

ANNE He's not a fellow, Dad. He's the man I love.

Pause.

Anyway, I've spoken to him and... You remember, at first,
when you came... How shall I put this? I'm wondering if
it wouldn't be better to... What do you think of this room?

Brief pause.

Mm? It's rather nice, isn't it?

WOMAN It looks on to the park.

ANNE Yes. It's very nice. It's like being in a hotel. Don't you
think?

WOMAN That's what all the residents say.

ANNE I think you might be better off here.

ANDRÉ Where?

ANNE Here. I was wondering if it wouldn't be more reassuring... nicer for you if we came to a joint decision that you should move in here.

Brief pause.

What do you think?

ANDRÉ What about you? What are you going to do? Where are you going to sleep? Which room?

ANNE If you remember, I'm going to go and live in London.

ANDRÉ No, you're not.

ANNE I am. Remember? I told you about it... Remember?

ANDRÉ But you said... Are you sure?

ANNE Yes.

ANDRÉ You told me you were staying here with me...

ANNE No, I have to go. It's important. I already explained it to you. But I'll come and see you. Occasional weekends.

ANDRÉ What about me?

ANNE You'll stay here. In Paris.

ANDRÉ All on my own?

Pause.

What about your sister? Where's she?

ANNE Dad...

ANDRÉ What?

Pause.

If you knew how much I missed her...

ANNE I do too, Dad, I miss her too. We all miss her.

ANDRÉ *takes a look at her, makes a gesture, perhaps even caresses her, as if for once he understood what can't be spoken.*

Pause.

Blackout.

Fifteen

A white bed, reminiscent of a hospital bed. ANDRÉ
doesn't know where he is. Then the WOMAN *comes in.*
She's wearing a white coat.

WOMAN Did you sleep well?

ANDRÉ What am I doing here?

WOMAN It's time.

ANDRÉ I didn't ask about the time. I asked what I was doing
here.

WOMAN How do you mean?

ANDRÉ Who put this bed here? In the middle of the drawing
room? Anne? This is really getting out of hand. I'm sorry
to say this, but it is getting out of hand.

WOMAN Don't get upset.

ANDRÉ I'm not upset. I'm just saying you don't put a bed in
the middle of a drawing room. It doesn't make any sense
at all. Where's Anne?

WOMAN Look, I've brought you your medication.

ANDRÉ Why don't you bugger off with your medication! What
are you, a nurse?

WOMAN Yes.

ANDRÉ *(finally realising who he's talking to)* Oh, you are...
Oh, so that's it... Oh, I see. You're a nurse...

WOMAN Yes.

ANDRÉ Oh, I see. That's what I was thinking. You're the type.
Typical nurse. So what are you doing here?

WOMAN Sorry?

ANDRÉ What are you doing here?

WOMAN Looking after you.

ANDRÉ You don't say! Looking after me?

WOMAN Yes.

ANDRÉ First I've heard of it. Since when?

WOMAN For quite a few weeks now.

ANDRÉ For quite a few weeks? I'm happy to hear it. Amazing! Nobody tells me anything in this house. It's always a fait accompli. I really need a little word with Anne. We can't go on like this. It's really starting to... But I thought we were getting a new one.

WOMSAN A new what?

ANDRÉ Nurse. A new nurse.

Pause.

The one who looked a bit like Élise. My other daughter.

Brief pause.

I met her the other day. Didn't I?

WOMAN All right. Will you take your medication?

ANDRÉ She was supposed to start this morning. Laura. Wasn't she?

WOMAN I think you're getting mixed up, André.

ANDRÉ The one who reminded me of Élise...

WOMAN *(impatiently)* Right.

ANDRÉ Yes, all right, fine. Let's take this medication. It's not timed to the minute, is it?

Pause. He takes his time.

What time is it?

WOMAN Time for your medication.

ANDRÉ I've lost my watch. You don't know where...? I've lost my watch... Anne? Anne?

WOMAN Your daughter isn't here, André.

ANDRÉ Oh? Where is she? Has she gone out?

WOMAN If you remember, your daughter lives in London.

ANDRÉ What? No, she thought about going. But in the end, it didn't happen.

WOMAN She's been living there several months.

ANDRÉ My daughter? In London? No, listen, it never stops raining in London.

WOMAN Look, yesterday, this postcard she sent you, we read it together. Don't you remember?

ANDRÉ What is this nonsense?

WOMAN Look.

She shows him a postcard. He reads it.

I tell you this every day. You ought to remember it by now. She lives in London because she met a man called Pierre, who she now lives with. But she comes to see you sometimes.

ANDRÉ Anne?

WOMAN Yes. Occasionally she comes for the weekend. She comes here. You go for a walk in the park. She tells you about her new life, what she's up to. The other day, she brought you some tea. Because you like tea.

ANDRÉ Me? I detest tea. I only drink coffee.

WOMAN But it's very good tea.

The **MAN** *comes in. He's also dressed in white.*

MAN Everything all right?

WOMAN Fine. We were just going to get dressed.

MAN Everything all right?

*ANDRÉ doesn't answer. The **MAN** hands a document to the **WOMAN**, which she signs.*

WOMAN There you are.

MAN Thanks. Have a nice day.

WOMAN See you later.

ANDRÉ Him, this one... Who is he?

*The **MAN** exits.*

WOMAN Who?

ANDRÉ Him... Who just left.

WOMAN That's Olivier.

ANDRÉ Olivier?

WOMAN Yes.

ANDRÉ Are you sure?

WOMAN Yes. Why?

ANDRÉ Nothing. But... How shall I put this? What's he doing here? I mean...in my flat. Do I know him?

WOMAN Yes. He's Olivier. You see him every day.

ANDRÉ Do I? And you...

WOMAN What?

ANDRÉ Sorry to ask this, but my mind's gone blank... I mean, you...you... Who are you, exactly?

WOMAN I'm Martine.

ANDRÉ Martine. That's right. Yes, yes, yes. Martine. And he's Olivier.

WOMAN Yes.

ANDRÉ Right. Right. And... What about me?

WOMAN What about you?

ANDRÉ Me... Who exactly am I?

WOMAN You? You're André.

ANDRÉ André?

WOMAN Yes.

ANDRÉ Are you sure?

WOMAN *(amused)* Yes.

ANDRÉ André? Nice name, André... Don't you think?

WOMAN It's a very nice name.

ANDRÉ My mother gave it to me. I imagine. Did you know her?

WOMAN Who?

ANDRÉ My mother.

WOMAN No.

ANDRÉ She was so... She had very big eyes. It was... I can see her face now. I hope she'll come and see me sometimes. Mummy. Do you think? You were saying she might come occasionally for the weekend...

WOMAN Your daughter?

He's crushed by sudden grief.

ANDRÉ No, Mummy. I... I want my mummy. I want my mummy. I want... I want to get out of here. Have someone come and fetch me.

WOMAN Now. Shush...

ANDRÉ I want my mummy. I want her to come and fetch me. I want to go back home.

ANDRÉ *starts sobbing. The* **WOMAN** *is surprised: she hadn't in any way anticipated this grief.*

WOMAN But... What's the matter with you? André... André... What's the matter with you? Come here. Come to me... Tell me what the matter is...

ANDRÉ I...

WOMAN Yes?

ANDRÉ I feel as if... I feel as if I'm losing all my leaves, one after another.

WOMAN Your leaves? What are you talking about?

ANDRÉ The branches! And the wind... I don't understand what's happening any more. Do you understand what's happening? All this business about the flat? You don't know where you can put your head down any more. I know where my watch is. On my wrist. That I do know. For the journey. If not, I wouldn't know when I might have to...

WOMAN First, we'll get dressed, shall we?

ANDRÉ Yes.

WOMAN We'll get dressed and then we'll go and have a walk in the park. All right?

ANDRÉ Yes.

WOMAN Good. All the trees. And the leaves. And then we'll come back here and have something to eat. In the refectory. Then you'll have a siesta. All right? And if you're on form, we'll take another little walk. In the park. The two of us. Because it's a nice day. Isn't it?

ANDRÉ Yes.

WOMAN The sun's out. We have to make the most of it. It doesn't happen every day. It never lasts very long when the weather's as good as this, does it? So let's go and get dressed, is that all right?

He clings on to her.

ANDRÉ　No.

WOMAN　Now. Don't be a baby. Come on. Come with me. All right? Come on. Easy. Easy. Shush. Shush. You'll be all right in a minute. You'll be all right. Shush...

He calms down, buried in her arms. She rocks him gently.

Pause.

Blackout.

PROPS

BACKSTAGE
USR PROPS TABLE
Shopping bag w. fake chicken and jacket potatoes
Anne's bag
Anne's keys
Laura's bag
Eaten chicken in dish w. cling film
2 x green and white tea towels, folded
3 x dinner plates w. Food dressing
Cling film
Bottle of red wine, full (no lid)

USR
Bed w. mattress
Sheet tucked in neatly
Duvet tucked in at foot and folded in half
2 x foam wedges
2 x pillows on top of wedges
Protective bed cover

USL PROPS TABLE
Clipboard w. Medical sheet
Pen
Uneaten chicken in dish w. cling film
2 x green and white tea towels, folded
Cafe au lalt cup w.
Uneatenmilk in plastic cup
2 x espresso cups (yellow and orange)
 1 x espresso cup (blue)
1x espresso cup (dark pink)
Sugar bowl
        w. Splenda
        Teaspoon
Yellow tablet box w. 3 x tablets in center section
Wine glass, half full
Mobile phone
Flask of coffee
Medical cone in glass w. water in plastic cup
Medical cup w. 2 x tablets

Newspaper
Pierre's glasses - clear glass, case open
Spare watch
Dumping table

ONSTAGE
Stage swept
Check for spillages/water marks
Check all marks inc. bed glow tape mark and DSC glow tape mark
Painting on wall
Kitchen door closed
Double doors open

KITCHEN
2 x kitchen units
LX plugged in to SR side of wall cabinet
On top of unit (SR to SL):
Tea towel hung on SR side of unit
Andre's watch on DSR corner
Toaster w. 2 x mugs in front
Kitchen roll
Water carafe, half full
      w. 3 x water glasses on top
Pile of tea towels
Cafetiere
Cutlery basket w. 3 x forks
      3x forks
      Serving fork and spoon
      Bin

USL
Desk chair swivelled to face audience
Desk on marks w. Glow tape on US of DS leg
      Telephone plugged in to 2 x socket
      Desk lamp plugged in
      Black tray w. Whisky bottle, 2/3 full w. stopper
      2 x whisky glasses
      Water carafe, half full
      Water glass
      Address book w. Andre's reading glasses , open

Gold box
DS drawer: 2 x pill bottles with big pills

DSL

Grey floor lamp on marks, plugged in, switch up
2 x armchairs on marks - SL chair w. glow tape on back
Coffee table on marks, glow tape US w. Newspaper in USL corner
Purple espresso cup in USL corner

DSR

Paper lamp on marks, plugged in, switch up
Dining table on marks, glow tape USC w. green trivet central 4 x dining chairs, tucked in

SR

London postcard blu tac'd to DS window frame
Bonsai tree on the centre of the window sill

USC

SR bookcase w. shelves full of books
       Black vase on top
       Blue vase on top
       Lower shelves (SR to SL)
Flowers in vase
Salt and pepper
4 x glasses
4 x placemats
4 x coasters
3 x water glasses
Lower cupboards (SR to SL)
       3 x whisky glasses
       4 x wine glasses
       Dressing
Lower shelves (SR to SL)
3 x napkins rolled in napkin rings
Grey vase, stuck down
Multi coloured bowl, stuck down
SL bookcase w. shelves full of books

USR HALLWAY
Coat hooks w. Andre's coat
Side table central to double doors w. Umbrella
Dish with coins 2 x pictures on wall (Dog SR, girl and dog SL)
Light flown in and line coiled

PERSONALS
Mr Cranham: Euros in money clip in PJs pocket
Mr Doherty: Glasses
Mr Flynn: Watch

LIGHTING

Blackout p8
Blackout p18
Blackout p27
Blackout p28
Blackout p36
Blackout p39
Blackout p40
Blackout p46
Blackout p48
Blackout p58
Blackout p60
Blackout p63
Blackout p68
Blackout p71
Blackout p78

SOUND EFFECTS

Bell rings P19
Doorbell p66
Doorbell p67

ABOUT THE AUTHOR

Florian Zeller is a French novelist and playwright. He won the prestigious Prix Interallié in 2004 for his third novel, *Fascination of Evil (La Fascination du pire)*. His plays include *L'Autre, Le Manège, Si tu mourais,* nominated for a Globe de Cristal, *Elle t'attend* and *La Vérité*. *La Mère (The Mother)* received a Molière Award for Best Play in 2011 and *Le Père (The Father)* received the Molière Award for Best Play in 2014, starring Robert Hirsch and Isabelle Gelinas (Molière Awards for Best Actor and Actress respectively). It received the Prix du Brigadier in 2015. *Une Heure de tranquillité (A Bit of Peace and Quiet)* opened with Fabrice Luchini, and has since been adapted for the screen, directed by Patrice Leconte. *Le Mensonge (The Lie)* was staged in 2015 with Pierre Arditi and actress wife Evelyne Bouix. His play *Avant de s'envoler* was produced during the 2015/2016 season, starring Robert Hirsch and Isabelle Sadoyan. This play has been produced in 2018 in the West End Wyndham's theatre starring Jonathan Pryce and Eileen Atkins, directed by Jonathan Kent under the title *The Height of the Storm*. His last play, *Le Fils (The Son)*, ends his trilogy. It has opened at the Comédie des Champs Elysées in 2018 under Ladislas Chollat's direction. It will be produced in Spring 2019 in London.

Image credit: Laurent Hini

ABOUT THE TRANSLATOR

Christopher Hampton became involved in theatre while studying French and German at Oxford University, and wrote a play in his first year. The Royal Court's production was so successful that it transferred to the Comedy Theatre while he was still a student, making him the youngest writer ever to have a play performed in the West End – a record which still stands. He said at the time that he also hoped to become the oldest writer to have a play in the West End, an ambition he has yet to achieve.

His plays, musicals and translations have so far garnered four Tony Awards, three Olivier Awards, five Evening Standard Awards and the New York Drama Critics' Circle Award; prizes for his film and television work include an Oscar, two BAFTAs, a Writers' Guild of America Award, the Prix Italia, a Special Jury Award at the Cannes Film Festival, Hollywood Screenwriter of the Year, and The Collateral Award at the Venice Film Festival for Best Literary Adaptation.

His works for the stage include original plays (*Appomattox, The Talking Cure, White Chameleon, Tales from Hollywood, Treats, Savages, The Philanthropist, Total Eclipse* and *When Did You Last See My Mother?*); plays adapted from novels (Ödön von Horváth's *Youth Without God*, Sándor Márai's *Embers*, Laclos' *Les Liaisons Dangereuses*, George Steiner's novella *The Portage to San Cristobal of A.H.*); musicals (*Sunset Boulevard, Dracula: The Musical* and, most recently, *Stephen Ward*, all with Don Black); libretti (*Waiting for the Barbarians, Appomattox* and *The Trial*, all with composer Philip Glass); and many translations (plays by Chekhov, Ibsen, Molière, Horváth, Yasmina Reza, Daniel Kehlmann and Florian Zeller; and a German musical based on Daphne du Maurier's *Rebecca*).

Hampton's screenplays include most recently *Ali and Nino* (based on the novel by Kurban Said), *Adore* (based on Doris Lessing's *The Grandmothers*), *A Dangerous Method* (based on his play *The Talking Cure*), *Chéri* (from the novel by Colette), *Atonement* (from the novel by Ian McEwan), *Imagining Argentina* (which he also directed), *The Quiet American* (from the Graham Greene novel), *The Secret Agent* (from Joseph Conrad's novel, and which he also directed), *Mary Reilly* (from Valerie Martin's novel inspired by Robert Louis Stevenson's *Jekyll and Hyde*), *Total Eclipse* (from his play of the same name, and in which he also performed), *Carrington* (the first film he also directed), *Dangerous Liaisons* (based on his play *Les Liaisons Dangereuses*), *The Good Father* (from the novel by Peter Prince), *The Honorary Consul* (from Graham Greene's novel), *Tales from the Vienna Woods* (from the von Horváth play) and *A Doll's House* (based on his translation of the play by Ibsen).

His television scripts include mini-series *The Ginger Tree* (from the novel by Oswald Wynd), *Hôtel Du Lac* (from the Anita Brookner novel), *The History Man* (from Malcolm Bradbury's novel), *Able's Will* and most recently *The Thirteenth Tale* starring Vanessa Redgrave and Olivia Colman, based on the novel by Diane Setterfield.

Other recent plays include *Tartuffe* in the West End and *The Height of the Storm* at Wyndham's Theatre, London. *The Height of the Storm* is the fifth Florian Zeller play Hampton has translated, following *The Mother, The Father, The Truth* and *The Lie*.

Image credit: Jill Furmanovsky

**Other plays by FLORIAN ZELLER published
and licensed by Concord Theatricals**

The Mother

Other plays by CHRISTOPHER HAMPTON published and licensed by Concord Theatricals

Art

Conversations After A Burial

A Doll's House

God of Carnage

Hedda Gabler

Les Liaisons Dangereuses

Life x3

The Mother

The Philanthropist

Savages

Tales From Hollywood

The Talking Cure

Three Sisters

Treats

The Unexpected Man

The Wild Duck

CPSIA information can be obtained
at www.ICGtesting.com
Printed in the USA
BVHW041413300421
606044BV00008B/380